Copyright © 2024 awakenAdream®

.all rights reserved.

Thank you for supporting creativity and the benefit of all beings.

PUBLISHED BY GROOVYROADS®
edited by Susan Rhodes

No part of this book may be reproduced, distributed, or transmitted
in any way, shape, or form by any means electronically nor mechanically,
including photocopying, recording,
or by any information storage and retrieval system.
All images and text may not be reproduced by any publisher, printer, or
company for the purpose of sale.

creatively written and illustrated from dreamAwake
images inspired from canva designs

.first printed edition 2024.

ISBN 978-1-963012-20-0

.cheers to all beings.

~awakenAdream, dreamAwake~

www.awakenadream.com

AWAKEN LIFE'S

GOLDEN TOOLS

dreamAwake
invites

———————————————

to Awaken Life's Golden Tools

Some moments have twists and turns
like a tornado.

Some days are calm and cool
like a cucumber.

Some weeks are filled with ups and downs
like a rollercoaster.

Emotions (energy in motion) are like the ocean
filled with calm waters of
joy, happiness, or love,
and gnarly waves of
anger, sadness, or anxiety.

Life's golden tools are with you always,
cheering for you
every moment, day, and week along the way.

Emotional health
is the grandest wealth.

GOLDEN TOOL
Hydrate

Water supports each heart throb,
encouraging clear skin,
assisting digestion to begin,
boosting energy levels,
and healthy brain vessels.
Hydrate like it's a fulltime job.
The body is 70% h2o.
Every cell in the body thrives on water. Yo!
Drink water like a camel,
after all you are a mammal.
Cheers to h2o!

GOLDEN TOOL

Nourish

Eat nutritious sustainable food,
it greatly affects your mood.
Processed food is a mess,
dyes create distress.
It is wise to know how food is created.
Ingredients must be clearly stated.
Be mindful of what you consume,
and never assume.
The body is a temple,
honor its needs.
It is that simple!

GOLDEN TOOL
Breathe

When in doubt,
breathe in and breathe out.
Breathing is the relaxing way.
Happiness is only a breath away.
Improve oxygen flow to the brain and body as you wish
or use the breath to blow bubbles like a fish.
Breathing enhances emotional well-being to thrive.
You are alive!

GOLDEN TOOL

Create

Art is great!
Enjoy the world of creativity,
paint, draw, tie dye, or choose any artistic activity.
Add color to the norm,
be like a chameleon and transform.
Focus on what you make,
it is your masterpiece to celebrate!

GOLDEN TOOL
Celebrate Nature

Venture outside and hug a tree,
leave technology inside and be free.
Plant a seed and watch it grow,
blossoming to create a natural show.
Share a smile with flowers
and dance with rain showers.
Enjoy the shining sun,
celebrating nature is great fun!

GOLDEN TOOL
Have Fun

Cards, dice, board or ball game,
perhaps design one with a new name.
Alone or on a team,
either is a playful dream.
Teamwork makes the dreamwork.
Play inside or outside
with fun as the guide.

GOLDEN TOOL

Music

Vibration is the word
with every note that is heard.
Sing a song like a bird.
Instruments create the tune,
dancing from the wind to the
moon.

GOLDEN TOOL
Meditation
Mindfulness strengthens self awareness. Surfing the waves of emotion, transforms the mental commotion. Meditation and relaxation calms any situation.

GOLDEN TOOL

Love

Be comfortable in your shell,
love yourself and be well.
The heart is where love begins.
Kindness always wins.
Live to love and love to live
is a grand positive.

GOLDEN TOOL

Movement

Stretch, yoga, dance, or exercise,
the mind and body will thank you and energize.
Enhance each moment
with lively movement.
Enjoy a stroll along a trail
and consider the journey of a snail.
Grooving forward,
joyously moving onward.

GOLDEN TOOL

Connect

Chat with plants, animals, or a friend,
any being who may comprehend.
Perhaps a sloth who is patient and lovable,
remember with magic, grace, and a steady
pace...anything is possible!
Let life flow
and enjoy the rainbow.

GOLDEN TOOL
Imagination

Awaken a dream,
dreaming awake is supreme.
Create an extraordinary project,
reduce and reuse any object.
Birdhouse, fort, maze, or marble run,
creativity with passion is a project well done.
Your imagination
is a spectacular illumination.

GOLDEN TOOL
Laugh

Laugh wildly like a chimpanzee

and you shall see,

laughing is joyfully freeing,

improving mental well-being.

Releasing neuropeptides* and reducing stress,

smiling or laughing is personal success.

Laugh out loud or smile

to go the extra mile.

*neuropeptides-chemical messengers in the brain

GOLDEN TOOL
Journal

Pencil, pen, marker, or chalk,
inspire paper to talk.
Allow words to flow
and thoughts to come and go.
Write, doodle, or draw it out
and feel your relaxation sprout.
Express your awesome self
and boost your life's health.

GOLDEN TOOL

Rest

Life tip from a koala bear,
rest and repair.
Sleep is required
to be free from growing tired.
Catch some zzz's,
if you please.
Gift the body time to reboot
before the daily commute.
Rest your mind,
give yourself the grace to unwind.

GOLDEN TOOL

Gratitude

Each moment be thankful,
celebrate life and live grateful.
Enjoy all the day brings
to fly and spread your wings.
Soar to grand heights,
rising with the sunlight
and dancing in the moonlight.

Celebrate life!
Live your best life.

GOLDEN TOOLS

Hydrate :: Water is Life
Nourish :: Nourishment fuels Life
Breathe :: Breathing is the essence of Life
Create :: Life is a creative journey
Celebrate Nature :: Life sprouts from the earth
Have Fun :: Enjoy your Life
Music :: Life sings from vibrations
Meditation :: Be in the present
Love :: Love the Life you live
Movement :: Groove with Life
Connect :: Share your Life with others
Imagination :: Imagine your best Life, live it!
Laugh :: Life is beautifully silly
Journal :: Express yourself
Rest :: Recharge your Life being
Gratitude :: Attitude of gratitude

www.ingramcontent.com/pod-product-compliance
Lightning Source LLC
Chambersburg PA
CBHW042039050526
44107CB00107B/1039